Vulnerable
More than feelings

By Khadijah Pratt

Copyright © 2021 by Khadijah Pratt, Britni Purcell
All rights reserved. This book or any portion thereof may not be reproduced or used in any manner whatsoever without the express written permission of the publisher except for the use of brief quotations in a book review.

Printed in the United States of America

First Printing, 2021
Illustrator: Britni Purcell

ISBN 978-1-7366626-0-1

Dedication - "For those of us who think and love deeply" - KP

She is a beautiful woman stripped down not only of her clothes but also her soul. She is deep within the surface and far above. She is as free as the whitest of doves. She is a warm spirit. Her aura is soft and full of bright colors. Her dark brown eyes are full of wonder. She is a beautiful woman stripped down not only of her clothes but also her soul. Her dark brown skin is full of melanin. Her hair is as knotty as her personality. She is a beautiful woman stripped down not only of her clothes but also her soul. She's vulnerable and naked to the earth she connects with. She is straight from the land we call our motherland. She's beautifully different, because she's naked, vulnerable, and open.

Find strength in your vulnerability.

Love and Passion

Sometimes on your path you may encounter times where you are tested on your love for others whether it's with family, friends, and even lovers. Also, to feel passion and love for someone even through the pain and sacrifice is very rewarding. Always keep your heart ready to accept love and lessons and you will never have to look back and regret the past. Continue moving forward and allow yourself to feel love and be loved. You deserve that much.

Your heart
Is like a reflection
Of what mine shows
They both kind of glow
Tainted with black spots
From many previous losses
These spots are little battle scars

My heart
Is like the same image
Of what yours shows
They both have sorrow
Tainted with dark spots
From all the hurt life caused
But fortunately it makes us who we are

Our hearts
Are like mirroring hands
That somehow take hold
And make the friendship grow
Still tainted with life's big falls
We stay on the rollercoaster until it stops
Because we both want to win life's cruel war

To lead with passion and love is to understand the good and bad that comes with it.

Like the powerful Sun's rays
Laughter pours out of my body
Like soft, genuine waves
Cheeks part like the Red Sea
Your smile is now the star of the show
There's an applause in my eyes
Fireworks erupt in my stomach
Like its a barbeque on the 4th of July
As a new heat wave spreading on Earth
Like eager thighs do on the first date
Colors emerge in the sky other than blue
As if anything else in the moment matters
Other than the Summer inside of you
It's the forgotten two months of the year
Where it comes when you wish for it
    But disappears as if it never existed…

Your love is like the months of Summer
I don't want you to go anywhere
I soak up the sun in the sky
Until the moon indicates it's night

During the day, I lay in the sand in sweat
Soft on my skin but hardens when wet
The waves thrust in between my thighs
A grand entrance of pure pleasure to rise

Your invitation to come closer
To feel all of you is all a drunken blur
I still remember your arms like when warm winds
Fiercely swirl around me, urging me to sin

Each day with you was like a sweet dream
And every night was like a sweaty fantasy
But just like Summer when the heat dies
All I'm left with is Winter's frozen tears in my eyes

Let me ride the vibes on your wave
                I want your words to take me away
And spin me around and around
                Like a carousel my mind goes
Until I'm back into your embrace
                Dancing is more like a chase
I follow your every move
                Allowing my hips to sway
I stare intensely into your eyes
                There's nothing you can hide
I speak to the king in you
                Without saying a single word
The wind blows through my mane
                I feel free, it drives me insane
I laugh as we move on autopilot
                We merge and become one unit
I feel your body like it was mine
                I hear your thoughts in my mind
I sense the universe of emotions
                They run through me like a current
I close my eyes to get lost in them
                Taking them in like they belong to me
I hold on to you like you've instructed
                To dance to the words, you've constructed

Let the words dance inside of my ears, like a ballerina.

I must say I've missed you every single day.
The closeness, the understanding; our bond.
It was apparent when you called upon me
that you wanted to speak on what's troubling
All I wanted to do was hold you closer to my heart.

Lay your head on my chest where you'll be safe.
You can listen to my heartbeat's slow rhythm.
Feel how I much I still want and crave your devotion,
The quicker it goes, the more you trace on my skin.
I lose myself as your fingertips paints me like art

If your fingertips are as dangerous as I remember,
then I'm gonna be in trouble and so will you.
Passion and love were never a problem for us
But the aftermath of emotions mixed with lust
Could start something so destructive
even our world isn't prepared for

You were always my safe place and my saving grace.

Water my mind like a flower and watch me grow to love you.

The room is filled with your scent

Even when you go away

You are still forever present

My body is used to your hands

Your fingerprints are permanent

You picked me in the bed flowers

The dandelion amongst sunflowers

Different but never lonely, I stood tall

You wanted to be in the middle of it all

By blowing away the seeds to see "me"

The parts that I was embarrassed to be

You kissed away my worries to be perfect

You made me realize my flaws were worth it

Turning all my doubts into affirmations

Making time for me like it's always a special occasion

Skin on skin action like you worship me,

Bowing down to adorn me at my feet

Even as your scent fades from my sheets

I smile as I get ready for the day

I'm running on no sleep but I'm wide awake

I traveled through different gardens collecting flowers that reminded me of you.

The passion I feel when I'm with you is like listening to a song for the first time. I focus on every part of it. From the vocals to the instruments. As if a song could caress my skin. You are my new favorite track that I've stumbled upon. I repeat you in my mind as it wanders, yearning to listen again and again. With each listen, I experience a different emotion. Joy, Sadness, and Pain are louder than the others. They're all the things I sense when I listen to your words. They are my personal lyrics that I remember. One of the things I find beautiful is your dark browns. There is more to explore beyond them coffee grounds. I hope one day I get to see hidden truths in your crown. Show me the tapes of the voices that pull you down. Allow me access to your gems. The way you think is birthed from a rough place, priceless like diamonds. You are music in human form, valuable to me. You are the song that haunts my dreams.

You are the song that I put on repeat.

When I look at the sky, I see our future.

Every morning I would walk outside
To count all the clouds in sight.
That day those white figures were
A puppy, a man, and an infant.
As always, I simply admired them.

Alone I stood as children played.
In the green grass I then lay.
I looked at the sky again in awe.
The clouds then changed again:
A car, a church, a mansion.

All those clouds became clear.
They were things I wanted for my future.
The reality of those clouds was raw.
Things that I've only dreamed about.
Unfortunately, the sun had to fade out.

The next day I walked outside,
I spotted a man sighing at the same sky.
He turned around sensing my presence.
Beckoning me to come closer,
He points at the sky's poster.

For some odd reason I then realized
why we were using the same eyes.
Why the children weren't so interested in our findings.
I knew right then what my future was gonna be
With the person who understood
    the same pictures of these shapeless clouds as me.

You never know who will stumble into your life. Remember to keep your heart open.

Sorrow and Compassion:

Sometimes on your path you may encounter dark thoughts and even bad situations, but you must remember that to get through these emotions, you must let them flow through your body and replace them with love. Remember that bottling up your emotions can lead to sleepless nights and even depression. You must fight through this because, in the end, pain is transient. Think about what makes you happy. Find your way through the darkness into the light. You deserve that much.

Long nights
Short days
pile on me
Losing time
Losing energy
No sleep.
Staring at the flat ceiling
Lights off, air blowing
Round and round
the fan goes
Silent, no replies.
Suddenly, I heard a voice
Whispering my name
and that was enough.
Then, I realized
where it was leading.
Outside of my room
It loudly whispered
over and over.
It called as I roamed
the empty hallways.
Then, I came to a stop
when I saw the staircase.
The voice said "jump"
and I followed it;

But that wasn't
the death of me
An angel swooped down
and caught me
in its arms.
The light was shocking
And for a second
I couldn't breathe
"Shhh, God sent me to protect you "
As I gasped for air
everything went black
and the angel disappeared.
Days go by
and it becomes normal again
Just a shadow of darkness
No voice
No angel.
Long nights
Short days
Pile on me
Losing time
Losing energy
My soul is asleep

Your sweet words of nothing
That you whispered to me
Caused me to fall in love with your lies,
Allowed me to drown in your kisses,
And get lost in your eyes.

It began when you were first introduced to me.
I was stunned because of your beauty.
You smiled when I couldn't speak properly,
As if you knew you were something special.
That should've been the first sign to leave.

But as time went by, the walls around my heart
Soon began to fall, and you began to pick it apart.
I was blinded by your sweet seduction.
The toxin called love was killing me softly,
But you still fed more into my infatuation.

Every sweet "I love you" that you whispered
Was washed away by sleeping with another.
My heart was completely torn in half
When I walked in on you in between her thighs.
It's going to take a lifetime to glue it back

Because your sweet words of nothing
Swept me away powerfully
Caused me to fall in love with your lies,
Allowed me to drown in your kisses,
And get lost in your seductive eyes.

Follow your heart but also never forget your intuition.

You are a precious gift that needs to be handled as such.

My soul burst with desire
It's because you lit my fire
You touched deep within me
As if I had a great awakening
You possessed me with a kiss
Took me hostage with your lips

Locked me in your cage of promises
Whispers of the future, a sweet hiss
You captured me in your embrace
Like a fly in a web unable to escape
You were my beautiful spider
Ready to eat my heart for dinner

You made it so I couldn't move
I was under your spell like a fool
Lust, Love, and Longing surrounded me
Like mango perfume you thought it was sweet
I felt exotic as you sucked it all in
As if taking over my body was a win

And so, you took over my everything
Sucked to the last drop what was left of me
I was left lying in a shimmering daze
Half shocked and half amazed
But just like the great love stories
You had achieved your happy ending

Then you left me behind so battered
Searching for your gaze in every man I've encountered
Poisoning every man who dared look my way
I've learned from the best of
    How did a fairy like me turn into a succubus?
    The girl who was taught by her captor to be just as wicked

To lead with understanding, you will be at a place of peace.

the feeling of emptiness returns
as the darkness fills me up at night
to be empty is to be whole in the soul
is what this love feels like

it's a poisonous feeling in my heart
that wraps itself around my neck
choking me until I can't breathe
forcing my lips open for a peck

a kiss from you is a kiss of death
it's so inviting and yet so cold
for you beckon me with that smile
to ensure that I will eagerly follow

toxins lay eggs in my system
itching inside but I scratch my skin
you tell me that it's normal to feel pain
while loving someone like a villain

you tell me that I'll never recover
that I'll never find someone new
but I'm being slowly manipulated
and forced to only find comfort in you

you're the monster I'm running from
the one I check under the bed for
yet I cling to you like you're my angel
even though you turned me into a demon

Your love was like sweet poison,
so bad for me and yet
I yearned for you with every breath.

I've been let down once again
Being used should be exhausting
'Tired' is only an understatement

'I wanted this', I say to myself
'I wanted this and now I've got it'
I've been taken off the shelf

I watched as he stamped his name
I was branded with the stroke of a pen
I was returned with ruined pages

I was past due but he paid the fees
He enjoyed himself as he read me
I only kept his attention for a week

He skipped the main chapters to finish
Didn't even try to get the main idea
Just rushed, only to get to "The end"

When one book ends, do not reread.

I could say things like you were the earth to my sun, but truthfully you were none of those things. You gave me the best laughs and the worst cries I ever had. You were intense yet gentle. You gave me breath but then you quickly took it away. I felt danger and yet I was secure when you held me tight. I knew this was wrong but still I held on. I knew one day I would have to let go, but to me you were my only home. I had nowhere else to go. You were it. All my fears that I bottled inside were silent. You were what people call an addiction. Like a person on drugs, I knew I shouldn't take the next hit. But you gave me that uncontrollable itch. You continued to nudge me closer to the edge. Close enough to see how far I climbed, but safe enough to take any backward steps. You never told me to save myself. You truly were the devil in the flesh. A tempter if there was such a being. You wore a mask to hide the beast. That illusion soon shattered to show your scarred face. I just couldn't look away. I was so far gone that I continued to love you, my only sin. Thinking that maybe you would put the mask back on and pretend once again. You never once put it back on for me. And through it all, I thought I mattered more like you once claimed. I guess to you, I was just a pawn in your game.

You kept me close to the edge; so when you saved me, you would be my superhero.

Love is an action verb, do it anytime you can.

Dark all around
As she hugs herself.
The wind blew harder
And got cooler
as the sun went down.

It was too late to play outside.
But her mother wasn't in sight
And it was a beautiful night.
She chuckled as she strolled
Thinking about when he'd show.

Park benches were scattered
Giving her the best privacy.
She surveyed the stars above.
Too young to have a boyfriend
But not too old to hide him.

A huge shadow loomed over her.
Then she felt a warm hand
Touch her waist and her privates.
She tried to make a sound
But nothing came out.

The hand got rougher and rougher
and pushed her to the ground.
He reached for her pants.
His hand stripped her bare
as she laid there.

She tried to tell him no
But he wouldn't let go.
She struggled and struggled
Trapped in his presence
 As he took her innocence.

Then she began feeling something
hard between her legs.
It plunged down her private.
Deeper and faster the pace
more tears fell on her face.

Finally it released from her body
Leaving her cold and wet.
Red blood soaked the grass.
As she pulled up her pants
He returned a shadow as he left
 and she wept.

Feelings churn in her stomach
The dark sky mirrored her thoughts
Those thoughts flood her body and mind
As she grieved the last piece of innocence

Self-love and Reflection:

Sometimes on your path you may encounter moments when you feel like you are not where you are supposed to be. It's normal to have those thoughts and feelings but in learning to accept and love your flaws, you will be the best version of yourself. You deserve that much.

She's a sage in this vacuous world
Many thoughts cloud her mind
To understand each thought
You would end up getting lost
Forever trapped in her cavernous mind
But diamonds are what you might find

She's not only an enlightened one
She's emotionally warm like the sun
Suffers just to experience empathy
Connect and she feels you physically
She seems fragile but she's not breakable
She's stronger than steel and marble

Her strength comes in different forms
Vulnerability is one of her configurations
She's willing to feel everyone and everything
Soft isn't the word that describes her bravery
Never underestimate her will to inspire another
She thrives on love and the serving of others

You can find her walking along those busy streets
I promise that you'll feel her like a warm breeze
Stop and say hello, find out for your own sake
You might even feel glorious for no reason
That's the effect she puts out in each season
Because genuine people are so hard to find
Look closely, you can see it with your own eyes

To lead with self-love, you will learn that you are a diamond within. You are your own best friend.

Take your time to find your true self. There is no need to rush

Mirror Mirror

on the wall

tell me

who's the failure

of them all

be gentle with me

let me down easy

I'm a little broken inside

every day I continue to lie

not only to myself

but everyone else

and I simply don't know why

all my feelings are piling up inside

so if you ask what's wrong

I wouldn't be able to answer at all

I'm nothing but flawed

Look at the mirror one more time
as I help get rid of the lies
you say your heart is broken inside
Here, I lend you mine
As long as you have my heart
you will be out of the dark
you see what you want
but I see who you really are
you give me light
when it's dark
you comfort me
when I feel lost
so, if I asked the mirror
to tell me who
is the greatest of them all
the mirror will shine
on your wonderful flaws

I am open
Like an old book
Full of controversy
Full of cuts and slits

I let the air in,
Like loose windows
The wind overwhelms me
I am naked and cold

I am also closed,
Like a finished diary
Full of sweet secrets
Under lock and key

I am a guarded door,
One step to my heart
you could get hurt,
Bruised, or torn apart

I am cautious,
Like a deer in the woods
I am quiet, I am aware
Of predators as prey should

But I'm also reckless,
I show my heart effortlessly
Like a woman in love
I am careless and clumsy

I am truly a door,
That is securely closed
But with the right key
I am open like a pot of gold

Dear Queen, Dear me

Hello, it's me again. I just wanted to use this platform

To give thanks to the Lord for the woman you've become

He took his time on you. He made you and all that you are.

And he is still molding and growing you into something more.

When I look at you, I see a beautiful woman and I love the view.

I'm so happy that God gave me sight so I can see your spirit glow.

Even at times when you feel awful, you're so strong and powerful.

You have many layers: I love your hard exterior and mushy interior.

You're able to help those you love and still save room for yourself.

You make time to look back and reflect on yourself

Queen, did I forget to mention your contagious smile?

The very one that warms even the coldest of souls

You are truly a treasure, a whole chest of jewels

Queen, I have to say you are truly inspiring.

You remind me that anyone could change.

Even the little girl with low self-esteem,

could find happiness within her being.

Yours always,

Me

Learn to unleash the queen in you and you will be treated as such.

The mirror only shows a small part of who you are. Look into your heart for the rest.

Soft as a pillow her heart is
one look at her and I understand
the pain, the feeling of hopelessness
yet I feel her fight, her willingness to stand
even when knees weaken
I sense her fears, if only I could silence them
and set her free from whatever binds her
I feel her feelings flow through me as if they are my own
the good and the bad, the happiness and the pain
because as I touch the mirror, I realize something
this girl I describe and I are one and the same

You are an incomplete painting so always be kind to yourself

An incomplete canvas, you are
a woman of many vibrant colors
But some are more prominent

Blue is the most noticeable hue
where your painting is consumed
Your loyalty is transcendent

Pink is one that outlines the corners
the veiled parts of you, the undiscovered
Warm, affectionate like no other soul

Indigo is my favorite trait that you own
your intuition, your endless wisdom
It's the most beautiful one that glows

Last but never the least, the color of your irises
you're down to earth like Osiris
A true definition of your individuality

You see, the most beautiful thing
is that you aren't even done growing
The color green surrounds this masterpiece

Never change yourself to fit a standard, you are too magical to be anyone else.

Allow your colors to show. Allow yourself to glow.

Hope and revelation:

Sometimes on your path you may encounter moments where life can bring you down. Trust the process and trust yourself. Be willing to ask and receive help and words of motivation from others. You deserve that much.

I take your hand in mine,
Urging you to close your eyes,
Whispering it's going to be alright,
Erasing all the concerns and lies.

Right now, you will feel pain.
But it will heal someday,
No more stomach aches,
Just my kindness to keep you safe.

Relax your mind.
Think of sunny days
and blue skies,
Because soon it will be okay.

Lead with faith and trust, you will always find yourself on the right path.

How many frogs do I need to kiss
until you're the only one I'm with?
How many heartbreaks do I endure
until you are mine and I'm all yours?

When will you take me by the hand,
realize that you gotta take a chance?
When are you gonna open your heart,
so I can be there when you fall apart?

Will you let me touch your soul with mine?
Like two birds sharing their food outside,
let's feed each other's minds, let's explore
and make love and make up over and over.

I wanna know all of you, not just your beauty.
I'll show you my darkness only if you show me
and we can play in the dark together like children.
That's only if you're down to answer my question.
       How many frogs do I need to kiss
       until you become my true Prince?

I'm longing to get to know you and spend my life with you.

We all need to be showered with love and happiness.

We're all in need of love fused with attention.
We live in a world where we need validation.
What happened to looking for similar souls?
We're just worried about coppin' new clothes,
Claiming that we're only savages and ice cold.
But what happens when that shit gets old?
When we're older and we have no wisdom,
All we got is a bunch of selfies, no experience
In careers that we slid into with confidence.
But we come home, with a phone in each hand,
Forgot a birthday on the mobile due to too many notifications.
Who uses Facebook when you're so used to the disconnection?
Fell victim to distraction, our shiny things.
Playing with our toys, the addictions we feed regularly, we need our fix to exist.
I'll speak for everyone by saying we're full of it.
Where can I find real authentic conversations?
Two people engaging in a couple questions,
Not even worried about the clock ticking.
What happened to searching for what makes us happy?
We live in a world where we "like" to relate
But I need to feel something,
                        anything
                        mundane…

Have you ever felt so mentally fatigued,
Carrying other's issues on your shoulders,
Loving them so intensely, that it hurts?
Self-care, you never even heard of it.
Self-love was a myth you read about in books.
The strain is showing up in your looks.
Deeper, the pain dug you in a huge hole.
In the black, you've buried yourself alive.
Your emotions are at an all time high.
You start to panic because you can't breathe.
Your friends add more into the mound,
while your family tells you not to break down.
The pile gets bigger and hard to hold.
Your problems clump up like spitballs.
Your aching hands are too full to carry it all.
But if you took the time to unload
all of the burdens of the ones you adore,
the blessings you blocked could be restored.

Empathy could lift you up or drown you. You decide.

I felt like I misplaced you in my head
I looked up and the presence of you dissipated
I couldn't hold you when I was lonely or sad
You were what kept me moving, now I'm idle
What once was or what could be is now erased
Without your precious light, how can I smile

I searched and longed for you in the stars at nightfall
When the world went without words or sound
The quiet filled me, for comfort I take part in alcohol
Moscato hit my taste buds and then I felt free
What was in my glass didn't prepare me for what I found
Pieces and pieces created a whole puzzle of me

I pulled out a small pocket mirror out of my purse
My reflection stared back at me with intensity
It was a true awakening, a blessing and curse
I laid in the grass with the wine half empty beside me
Memories of when I first fell apart consumed my being
My eyes heavy, I looked up at the sky again and knew
                who God wanted me to be

Let the universe guide you and you will never be alone.

I hope these words will help you through your own situations like it helped me. Art shouldn't be just for the artist but for others to listen to your voice, your tears, and your experience. I hope you will keep fighting the demons that bring you down and understand that when you lead with love, you can get through anything.

With that being said, I leave you with one last piece that helped me learn how to lead with vulnerability

I fell for you faster than raindrops in a storm
I thought of you as the butterflies began to form
You still look just as beautiful as you did before
my handwriting on a legal pad that rhymes
Cursive and 12 pt font that I used all the time
you were what I call an inspiration love
I talked to you on my pull-out bed
wrote silently as my brother slept
Some people call it a hobby or talent
but I don't see it like others do
you were my everlasting breakthrough
You were the one thing I possessed
The treasure of words I've kept

THE END.

www.ingramcontent.com/pod-product-compliance
Lightning Source LLC
Chambersburg PA
CBHW041403090426
42743CB00006B/136